Where Our Food Comes from

Children's Agriculture Books

BABY PROFESSOR

EDUCATION KIDS

Speedy Publishing LLC
40 E. Main St. #1156
Newark, DE 19711
www.speedypublishing.com
Copyright 2016

Do you love eating?
What are your favorite foods?
Do you love to eat fruit, vegetables and meat?
Have you ever wondered where
these foods come from?
Do you know that farmers feed the world?

This book will help
you understand where
the food on your
table comes from.

Where do you think the food that we buy in the stores come from?

You're right! Our food comes from the farm. We should thank our farmers for giving us food .

Let's talk about farming
and agriculture.

Farming was first practiced by tribes that we changing from a nomadic to a settled life. Instead of roaming from place to place, they thought of making their food through farming. It was during the First Agricultural Revolution around 10,000 BC.

It was during this period that the "founder crops" of agriculture were developed. Hulled barley, peas, and emmer wheat are some examples of these so-called founder crops. Mechanized farming technology came much later, during the Industrial Revolution.

Agriculture is a way of growing crops and raising animals to provide great amounts of food. Today, farming has been made easier through the help of modern machinery and chemicals to create abundant harvests.

This is known as industrial farming. This kind of farming increases the amount of food produced. However, industrial farming is not safe for the environment.

This is the reason why
many people choose
sustainable farming
or organic farming.
Farmers following
organic farming have to
be careful in choosing
their crops to match
their soil and other
growing conditions.
Since they are not using
chemicals, farmers
have to be more
skilled in their work.

Farmers plan what to plant and the methods of planting in order to have a bountiful harvest. Organic farming does this too, but in a more nature-friendly way.

Do you know where plows were invented? When agriculture began in the Middle East, farmers invented the plow to help open the soil so they could plant their seeds. The first plow ever invented was known as an "ard".

Agriculture has an important role in our everyday lives. It provides our food and maintains our economy. Many people want to practice agriculture. Hence, there are many farmers in the world. In fact, in the United States of America, agriculture is one of the largest industries. Many Americans are farmers. They have good lives. Farming is their way of life. Many people are employed in the farm.

New technologies have made farming more productive and efficient. Farmers can produce a wide variety of crops because of modern farming. For this reason, we should be grateful to the farmers in the world for feeding us. They work hard on the farm to give us food.

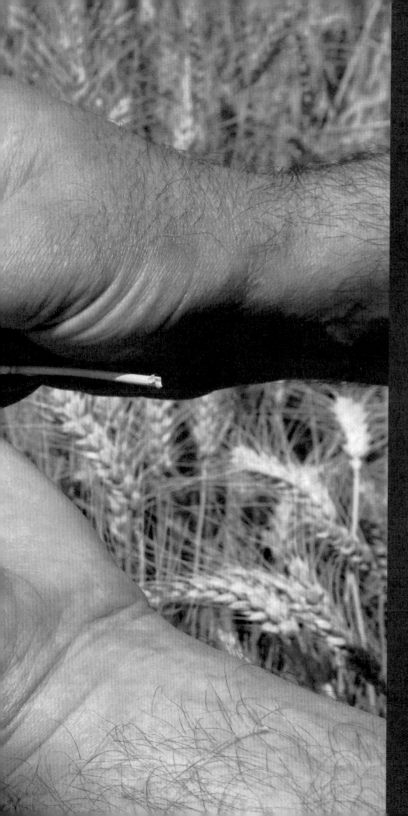

The food that we eat every day is made affordable because of efficient agriculture. Advances in technology have helped farmers in many ways. Developments in farming are seen in the quality of the soil, the crops and the harvest. More efficient farming methods have been used by farmers to assure good harvests. The planting, harvesting, storing, processing of farm products have been made easier than before.

Developments in agriculture resulted in larger harvests and better quality of crops or products.

What is the number one fruit crop in the whole world? Bananas are the number one fruit crop. In fact, bananas are the fourth largest crop in the world. Many countries in the world grow bananas. India leads all other countries in its banana output.

We get most of our food from the farm. Hence, farming and agriculture are very important in the society. If there were no farmers, we would have to get our food by hunting.

Agriculture is the backbone of the economy of many countries. It also provides employment to people. It provides a great way of living.

How about you? What
are your thoughts about
farming? Would like
to thank the farmers
for the food you eat?

58284335R00024

Made in the USA
San Bernardino, CA
26 November 2017